REBUILDING SELF-WORTH IN RECOVERY

New Morning, Second Dreams

By Cecil C.

CompCare® Publishers

2415 Annapolis Lane
Minneapolis, Minnesota 55441

Library of Congress Cataloging-in-Publication Data
Cecil C., 1899-
   Rebuilding Self-Worth in Recovery
     p. cm.
   ISBN 0-89638-256-7
   1. Self-respect 2. Compulsive behavior—Treatment
      3. Substance abuse—Treatment.
    I. Title

   RC489.S43C2 1992
   616.86'06—dc20   91-24076

                                 CIP

Cover design by Lois Stanfield
Interior design by MacLean & Tuminelly

Inquiries, orders, and catalog requests should be addressed to:
CompCare Publishers
2415 Annapolis Lane
Minneapolis, Minnesota 55441
612/559-4800
Toll free 800/328-3330

6	5	4	3	2	1
96	95	94	93	92	91

To my grandsons:
John, Larry, Randall, David, and Thomas

Contents

*L*ow self-esteem is one of the most pervasive and powerful deterrents to our progress in recovery from addiction. Recovery simply cannot proceed if we are not in touch with our self-worth.

Regardless of the circumstances and consequences of our addiction, we share a common bond with other recovering people when we work to rebuild self-worth. Fortunately, the road back to self-worth can be one of the most enriching journeys of our lives. The signposts along this journey are already known to us, but most of us need to take another look at them and consider their significance to our recovery and our sense of self. As a start, consider the principles suggested by each of the Twelve Steps: Acceptance—Belief—Faith—Honesty—Hope—Courage—Humility—Responsibility—Trust—Gratitude—Patience—Charity.

We need a program and ongoing support to help us rebuild self-worth as surely as we need a program and ongoing support to help us abstain from addictive behavior. Each of the fourteen chapters that follow focus on suggestions for rebuilding self-worth that has been compromised or destroyed by compulsion, dependency, or excessiveness. Throughout, it is emphasized that any substantive effort to regain self-worth must be "an inside job." Indeed, every addicted man and woman is told early in recovery that *no one can do it for you*.

But despite the reality that no one can do the work of recovery for another person, those who actively seek spiritual progress in recovery inevitably discover that *you can't do it alone*. The most successful route to self-worth is characterized by the process of caring and sharing with others.

This book is truly the result of sharing with others. I hope you will find it a useful reminder of the life-transforming concepts we learned and shared with each other in the early days of recovery. Consider it a brief refresher course as you continue your progress in recovery and attend to the vital issue of self-worth.

Cecil C.

We know what a person thinks not when he tells us what he thinks, but by his actions.

—Isaac Bashevis Singer

Act, Don't React

A young woman I know achieved six months of sobriety by confronting and overcoming many complex problems and coping with great emotional pain. Aware of this young woman's struggles, a well-wisher in her group shared this thought along with her congratulations: "Well," she said, "the Program saved our lives, but I guess we need to remind ourselves that it never promised us a rose garden."

The young woman's eyes sparkled as she responded: "Oh, but I believe this Program gave me a garden in which many rosebushes are *planted*. I think of my progress in the Program in this way: I must continue to work in my 'garden' to bring the plants to full and beautiful bloom. I know that if I want lovely roses, I must regularly pull weeds, water and nourish the plants, and do what I can to keep harmful things away from them. Only with this kind of sustained vigilance and effort will I have beautiful roses. And then, unless I'm willing to risk being stuck by a thorn, I'll never have the courage to gather bouquets from my garden as gifts for those I love."

In order to rebuild self-worth, we need to take action instead of passively waiting to react to conditions and situations in our lives. Action brings change. We relinquish control of our lives when we develop the habit of only *reacting* to outside stimuli. Until we confront, accept, and deal with adventures (and misadventures) as an integral part of our life experience, we will continue to be vulnerable to and victimized by influences outside our own thoughts and moods.

Action—not reaction—will always be the first choice of a person who participates fully in a program of recovery. We must act in order to deal with emotions that arise from exterior forces, or we will continue to falsely believe and behave as if we are victims. That belief, in turn, will make us even less effective in dealing with our own lives.

It is important for us to make constructive, positive choices in all areas of our lives. One simple example is the language we choose to define ourselves. For example, in describing our addiction and recovery, we can replace the negative statement "I can't use" with a pro-active statement "I can *not* use." By choosing active, positive concepts rather than passive, negative ones, we can prevent outside influences from gaining control of our emotions. While we can do many things to resolve our emotional problems, we can't do *everything*. Instead of reinforcing a passive stance by saying to ourselves "I'll never indulge again as long as I live," we can learn to focus on action instead and say, "I'll practice control one day at a time." Here's an important distinction to remember: in recovery we have not lost freedom to engage in addictive behavior but instead gained freedom *not* to engage in addictive behavior.

Much of our ability to act instead of react comes from studying the principles of our fellowship and persevering in our efforts to work the Twelve Step Program in all areas of our lives. This is why longevity in recovery should never be taken for granted or trivialized. If we remind ourselves daily that we are now living our lives by the principles of the Twelve Steps, we will find that self-esteem is more easily attained.

In recovery programs, people often are urged to strive toward a 180-degree change in attitude. When we come to realize that action rather than reaction is moving us toward that goal, we feel clearer and better about ourselves and our progress.

Sometimes, the action we take might be as simple as seeking a friend to talk with at a time when we feel unusually burdened or alone. When we take action and reach out in this way, we gain assurance that we have back-up support and that we're not facing a challenge or problem alone. This seemingly minor action can do wonders in helping us avert crises.

Constructive thinking can become habit-forming. Each and every one-day-at-a-time begins at the moment we make the decision to act. We will feel better about ourselves if we begin our days with constructive, positive thoughts. Each day is far too precious to poison it from the start with random feelings of negativism and inadequacy.

As recovering addicts, however, we know that we are only a slip away from returning to our active addiction. Boredom usually indicates a lack of involvement; it can lead to the stinkin' thinkin' we're not enjoying abstinence as much as our fellow recovering addicts because of some defect in *us*. Boredom can undermine self-esteem, but we can take simple action to deal effectively with it. When we begin feeling bored (and subsequently useless and unneeded) we can take action steps to become more involved with our recovery program. If we continue to be only *receivers* of the gifts of the program, we will surely experience boredom—and a subsequent erosion of our self-worth.

Without active involvement, even the most comfortable state of abstinence can become boring, then troublesome. It is not enough to attend Twelve Step meetings and read inspirational books. If we ever feel that we "have it made" in recovery, we need to look carefully at ourselves and our progress. Smug feelings of accomplishment and complacency in the program are real danger signals. Vigilance is a must, and vigilance requires action.

Carrying the message to other addicts is an important element of sustained recovery that requires action. Fortunately, this kind of activity is usually pleasurable and fulfilling. Among the rewards of Twelve Step involvement is the spiritual growth each member achieves by caring for and sharing with others. Indeed, giving voluntarily of ourselves to help others advances our spiritual growth and self-worth. Material rewards become meaningless to us when we volunteer our time to work with other recovering addicts. Among the rewards we receive when we give of ourselves is the recognition of genuine values in our lives. Working with others helps us see that the really important things in life are not those we can hold in our hands but those that fill our hearts—serenity, security, self-knowledge, and self-love.

Rarely will we feel self-hatred or boredom if we remember what many old-timers in the Program have told us: that we can do what medicine, justice, the courts, and organized religions have done with only minimal success. When we help others in the Program, and therefore help ourselves, we are actively involved in a dynamic that simply cannot tolerate feelings of low self-worth.

Develop the habit of acting to avert crisis rather than relying on delay or denial in the face of stress.

All fantasy should have a solid base in reality.

—Sir Max Beerbohm

Face Reality

good friend of mine enjoys sharing with others a memorable experience he had at his very first Twelve Step meeting years ago. At this meeting, a youth of nineteen with one year of sobriety shared his story with the group. The young man ended the story with this statement: "Today, because my Twelve Step group taught me to set goals and showed me how to work toward them, I'm convinced that I am the *best me* I've ever been." My friend, shaken by this young man's story, turned to the young woman sitting beside him, an "oldtimer" in the group even though she was a teenager. He said to this young woman, "God, how I wish I could say about myself what that young man just said about *himself*. But as I sit here tonight, middle-aged and supposedly in the prime of my life, I am without a doubt the *worst* me I've ever been." The young woman gently patted my friend's arm and said to him, "You will feel and say what he just did—when you stop living in a fantasy world of addiction and begin to face reality in recovery."

As we grow from addiction to sobriety, our orientation naturally shifts from fantasy to reality. But we must continue to focus on reality in all stages of recovery. As long as we live in a world of fantasy, we cannot grow in recovery, nor will we regain feelings of self-worth. We can save ourselves a significant amount of time, energy, and pain if we accept reality early in recovery. When we are grounded in reality, we can see that adversity does not destroy character defects, but *exposes* them instead.

When we face reality, we also face the fact that self-esteem is not a matter of bargaining with fate, or life, or other people, or even ourselves. Acceptance of what we were as addicted people and what we hope to become in recovery will never occur if we make our acceptance of reality contingent upon some return or reward. When we start any task leading toward spiritual growth, we gain little if we do not complete the effort. When we give less than we're capable of giving to an effort, we create anxiety in ourselves that could deter our growth.

But acceptance of reality marks only the beginning of our quest for self-worth. We need to *live* with reality in order to make progress. And living with reality means, among other things, that we can no longer live on the surface of our skin, that we cannot betray or manipulate people, then expect their forgiveness, and that we cannot plan our lives and set our priorities as if a pot of gold was just around the corner.

We will regain self-worth more quickly if we discard or downplay clearly *impossible* dreams early in recovery.

We have the best chance of building self-worth when we make an effort to *create* our own opportunities, rather than relying on fate, luck, or miracles to create opportunities on our behalf. Now, this doesn't mean that we can't afford to daydream in recovery. In fact, constructive daydreams plant ideas in our subconscious that we *can* succeed. Deeply inspiring and energizing daydreams evolve from reality-based goals. If we develop the habit of daydreaming about positive strengths like achievements, confidence, and a spirit of sharing with others, our conscious thoughts will begin to focus on success and take precedence over the thoughts of failure that preoccupy the addicted person's mind.

Reality also teaches us that giving to others without ego involvement adds to our self-worth. In recovery, we need to strive to give without ego, because ego is just another name for fear. If we are full of fear, guilt, or shame, we will not be capable of growing emotionally, even with a loving and giving attitude. Recovery that is based on these negative, energy-depleting feelings will not be effective for a significant period of time.

Attitudes and actions of forgiveness are essential in our search for renewed self-worth. We will never make spiritual progress if we spend time and energy judging others. Reality teaches us that genuine forgiveness involves a complete release of resentment, envy, and fear of others. Love and service become the substitutes for these negative feelings. How well the words love and service fit together: Love without service is a selfish act; service without love is an empty gesture. Love can be as simple as the act of accepting people, places, and things. As newcomers to our Twelve Step groups, we received reassurances of acceptance from others that carried us through some difficult times. They'd say to us, *"Let us love you until you can learn to love yourself."*

If we are burdened with feelings of unworthiness, love of self will be the hardest kind of love to achieve. To love lovable people is an easy task. But the true test of our ability to love will come from our efforts to love people we consider unlovable. How gratifying it is to see the unlovable become lovable simply because we make an effort to project love their way. And what could be more rewarding than experiencing our own unlovable selves becoming lovable because of a change in our attitudes?

Most addicted men and women are basically excessive people who suffer needlessly because they don't understand that more is not necessarily better. If we are to regain self-worth in recovery, we must give up the idea we once held that anything worth doing at all is worth doing to excess.

And since we're already addressing self-worth and reality, it is important to keep our emerging feelings of self-worth in perspective. We must live with others as well as with ourselves, or our quest for self-worth will be long, rough, and ultimately very lonely. Growth of our own feelings of self-worth should not prompt us to take charge of things when we participate with others. Overindulging in ourselves may actually deprive us of the help we need from friends in our recovery program—or at least it may cool the enthusiasm of others for us. We will progress when we learn from others, but first we must learn to peacefully coexist with them. Spreading our wings to show off the splendor we believe they possess may result in a strong self-image pleasing to us, but off-putting or offensive to others.

"Easy Does It" is not the complete answer in attaining self-worth that is devoid of arrogance and self-centeredness. But the slogan does contain one concept—patience—which is an important aspect of reality to consider when we slip back into compulsiveness and begin to want too much too soon. Caution is usually a deterrent for compulsiveness. Patient people rarely do or say "the utterly wrong thing" in their relationships with others.

In order to benefit from reality, we must believe that while we cannot control it, we *can* determine our attitude toward it. We need to remind ourselves that time is wasted when we spend it denying or bemoaning our fate or striving to avoid becoming what we do not want to be. The only sensible approach is an active and positive one—focusing our efforts on what we want to be.

Here's a fine example of a recovering person who faced a challenging reality and planned for it with a positive attitude: A very fine actress I knew had a particularly captivating voice that was widely heard from the stage, motion picture screen, television…and podiums at Twelve Step meetings. When she was well-established in her own recovery from alcoholism, this actress developed another life-threatening disease—cancer of the throat. Her condition resulted in several hospitalizations. When fellow group members visited her at bedside prior to her final surgery, she acknowledged the reality of her situation, then shared the plan she'd already devised: "The doctors tell me that even if this surgery is successful, I'll never be able to speak again. But my sharing days won't come to an end. I want to take lessons in sign language so that I can take hearing-impaired members to Twelve Step

meetings and interpret the Program for them."
Unfortunately, this lovely woman never got the chance to
realize these goals here on earth. But she died with the
gifts of recovery. Subsequently, three of her friends were
so inspired by her plan for sharing that they carried it out
with hearing-impaired people. That outreach continues to
this day. This woman's legacy was one of facing reality
with grace, a constructive dream, and a positive plan for
extending the spirit of sharing with others.

*L*earn to fully confront the issues and challenges of reality, don't just articulate them, tiptoe around them, or meet them half-way.

The greatest discovery
of my generation
is that human beings
can alter their lives
by altering attitudes
of mind.

—William James

Choose the Positive Approach

More than a century ago, renowned psychologist/ philosopher William James wrote extensively on the influence of the mind on the body. At that time, Dr. James also advanced the theory that actions profoundly affect thoughts and moods. Of course, the mind-body connection is well-established and supported today. But we need to remind ourselves frequently of the powerful relationship between positive thinking and positive action in every stage of life and recovery.

Think and act positively. This is essentially what we are being advised to do when, as newcomers to Twelve Step groups, we are told to follow the winners and work with the losers. A winner will readily say "I was wrong" when that is the case; losers almost always have knee-jerk responses based on a defensive stance that "*it wasn't my fault.*"

Actually, blamelessness is something only losers strive for, because it can be attained only through inaction. When we have negative attitudes about ourselves, we tend to rationalize by always blaming other people for our failures, disappointments, and disillusionments. Subsequently, we build up anger toward others and even begin to hate ourselves for having trusted other people at all.

Negative thinking activates self-pity and the related complaint of feeling "put upon." Newcomers to Twelve Step Programs are told that there is a world of difference between accepting problems and being *resigned* to them. The first attitude is full of hope, while the second is fraught with self-pity. There is perhaps nothing more important to self-worth than learning to recognize and choose the positive approach to tasks and problems.

If we seek growth in recovery, we need to *understand* negative thinking rather than fear it. Anxieties, along with self-pity, originate with overall negativism that turns us into "blame-throwers" at people, places, and things. When we have positive attitudes about ourselves, we are less likely to find fault with others. Positive attitudes provide a favorable environment for growth and sustained recovery.

We cannot rebuild self-worth when we are, as some have quipped, "always tied up in 'nots' spending our time and energy in the complaint department of life." Neither can we rebuild self-worth as long as we continue with our negative self-talk. We all know the telltale phrases: *"Yeah, but..."*; *"If only..."*; *"I ought to..."*; and *I'll try to...."* This kind of self-talk is amazingly powerful—it reinforces a mind set that can sustain a negative self-image indefinitely. Uncertainty about ourselves invites failure. It is, of course, much *easier* to think failure than it is to think success. Failure is simply not achieving a goal, while success is diverse and individual.

When our addiction led us to obsessive acts, it was easy to avoid all responsibility. At that time, we were sure that we were incapable of accomplishing *anything*. When we acted out as addicts, many of us essentially accepted failure as a form of punishment for our behavior. In recovery, we discover that responsibilities and commitments help to keep us sober, clean, moderate, and resistant to compulsions. And it follows that in recovery we must develop confidence that success, or at least satisfaction, will be the natural result of positive thinking and positive action.

A solid sense of self-worth doesn't come to us overnight, and positive thinking can help us consciously seek patience. Those of us who seek self-assurance, but feel discouraged by what we perceive as slow progress on our part, can take a lesson from expert mountain climbers: rarely do they look up at the great distances they have yet to go, but instead they keep themselves encouraged by turning, every now and then, to look down at the majestic vista below that represents the progress they've already made toward their goal.

Most of us can see happiness when we encounter it or when it surrounds us. But unless we develop confidence in the choices we make and learn to trust our instincts as well, we will never be able to *foresee* happiness. The real benefits of positive thinking will not come to us until we determine that we deserve them.

When we are free from addiction, we have the potential to learn and develop wisdom…and retain it as

Choose the Positive Approach

well. As our self-worth grows through positive thinking, we begin to understand that an overwhelming fear of the unknown, common to all addicted people, is a monster to us only because we have allowed it to be so. Instead of being frightened by the unknown, we can learn to look *forward* to the unknown, along with its unforeseen opportunities. In fact, we can learn to *welcome* the unknown by telling ourselves that it just might represent something that refreshes and/or enriches our lives.

When we develop confidence in our own positive thinking and intuition, we feel more assurance that we are people of significant worth, to ourselves and to others. As long as we continue to give time and energy to nagging feelings that we are somehow less than others, we cannot be constructive or productive. When we believe that we are not *destined* to fail, the idea of failure will have less prominence in our thinking and in our lives.

"Never better." This was the standard reply of a Twelve Step group member to the standard greeting ("How are you?") from other members of his group before and after meetings. Indeed, this man never failed to answer greetings with these same two words. At first, the people in his group accepted his reply as a mere pleasantry. But as weeks and months passed and the same reply continued to come from this smiling man, people began to hear something more in it: his seemingly automatic response was really a positive statement about living each day in recovery.

When a formerly helpless, hopeless addict lives with the security and serenity that abstinence brings, each day feels so new and rewarding that, truly, no previous day can surpass its beauty and opportunity. Earlier days may have been, year after year, just as glorious and worth living as "this day" but they were, in fact, *never better*. We will be more likely to cherish each day as the gift it is when we learn to live as if that particular day is all we have (and it is!). With a positive orientation guiding our thinking and our actions, we, too, can be *never better* each day.

Self-worth grows from our consistent use of good habits, while bad habits contribute to whatever bad feelings we have about ourselves. As we learn to develop the habit of positive thinking, it is important to remember the need to start each day with positive energy. If our days begin with love in our hearts and a spirit of sharing, we will have good and productive relationships with people. And when we make positive connections with people in our daily activities, we feel better about ourselves. Truly, *thoughts have wings*. We project our thoughts on others. If we live each day grounded in positive thoughts and actions, we will find that it is much easier for us to love ourselves. The seeds of self-worth are planted in just such a wondrously simple way.

*R*esolve to begin each new day with positive energy.

Growth is the only

evidence of life.

—John Henry Cardinal Newman

Open Your Mind to Personal Growth

One of the most important steps we take in rebuilding self-worth is making sure that we don't cling to the belief that we deserve *no* credit for our character growth. It actually impedes our progress when we tell ourselves that the positive changes we've made are a gift we received by simply expressing our needs and having faith. Too many of us continue to repeat (and believe) the words, "I can't take credit for my coping skills; my Higher Power gave them all to me."

It *is* true that each of us who managed to move from the depths of despair to serenity and security is a miracle of recovery. Regardless of how easy or difficult our growth process is, everything begins with a spiritual experience of some kind. This emotional awakening may vary from a sudden, dramatic insight to a hard-earned awareness of the realities of our basic problems. When we emphasize the idea that we were "gifted" with success, we risk adopting patterns of thinking that tell us we're merely "lucky." This mind set, in turn, supports the notion that we aren't required to extend ourselves in working for ongoing recovery and growth.

If we convince ourselves that our recovery is a blessed handout from God, we are in danger of assuming our Higher Power has taken pity on us and answered our prayers *because of our inadequacy to cope for ourselves.* When we look at things this way, we may be denying ourselves the joy of growing spiritually or interpreting growth as a true reward for our dedication and persistence. We will be more open to personal growth if we approach the task of rebuilding self-worth with the thought that we can accomplish good things *because we have a purpose in making the effort and have been provided with guidelines to follow.*

Enhanced self-worth will have no lasting value in our lives if we seek it merely because we feel it is expected of us or because it is a commendable goal. Instead, there must be a sincere and fervent wish on our part to grow emotionally and spiritually. Yet, we cannot experience renewed self-worth unless we believe it *can* materialize and that it *will* come about. In spiritual growth, the need for personal faith is obvious.

Another important step in rebuilding self-worth is fully accepting the fact that as addicts, we are victims of a disease. It really doesn't matter whether or not we consider ourselves active contributors to the progress of that disease or believe that we were victimized by addictive substances or behaviors. Many of us almost lost our lives to our addiction, yet never realized we were addicts. Somehow, *most* of us knew in our hearts that we were having difficulty controlling our behavior. We sensed that our addiction was altering our lives in harmful ways. We had almost daily proof that we were unable to resist compulsions or predict our behavior following the use of an addictive substance. Out of these realizations emerged our own ominous conclusion that we were weak-willed or immoral people in a world where the vast majority of people behaved differently than we did.

The fact that addiction is identified as a disease should signal us that engaging in self-blame is a useless exercise. Self-worth will begin to grow when we accept the fact that our excessiveness was not a symptom of weak will. Lack of will power had nothing to do with our slide into addiction, nor does will power figure prominently in our continued recovery. We learn early in our abstinence that we can no more will ourselves not to be obsessive than an insomniac can will himself or herself to fall quickly into a deep and lengthy slumber.

While it is helpful to know that a disease—and not a personal flaw or weakness—brought us to our personal low, we must guard against using the disease "defense" as an excuse or rationalization. We won't rebuild self-worth by telling ourselves that we were doomed from the start and never really had a *chance* for a normal life. Rationalizations are certain to derail any progress toward self-worth.

We must also guard against concentrating exclusively on self-knowledge in our efforts to rebuild self-worth. Self-knowledge is a valuable tool, but it does not necessarily lead to renewed self-worth. Personal inventories certainly represent a worthwhile step in our recovery. But self-knowledge and inventories do not necessarily lead to feelings of self-worth. In fact, an inventory could very easily lead us away from feelings of worth. When our inventories bring forth feelings of guilt and shame, we may find it difficult not to hate ourselves for what we were. But if renewed self-worth is our goal, we must focus on positive thinking and constructive action.

During our active addiction, most of us successfully purged ourselves of positive qualities, self-confidence, and self-respect. We transferred confidence from ourselves to an addictive substance or behavior, then began to believe that our compulsions pointed us toward pleasurable living. When we finally became aware of our enslavement to addiction, all of the early warnings we heard about obsessiveness and our former staunch avowals that "it will never happen to me" returned to haunt us. We realized that, not only had *it* happened to us, but our self-respect had disappeared as well. The resulting feelings of guilt, shame, failure, humiliation, anger, rejection, self-pity, and other self-defeating emotions worked together to maintain our low self-esteem.

If we are to be effective managers of our lives following our surrender to reality, we must recapture and reinforce a positive image of ourselves as *winners* in the battle against a powerful foe. Our self-worth has been badly damaged, but we can grow emotionally, even as that damage is being repaired. We need to affirm ourselves as we use the tools that our recovery program provides. We must believe that we are *worthy* of winning. We will find the confidence we need in the advice of those who have become winners before us.

We will regain lost self-worth if we focus less attention on avoiding character defects and negative emotions and more attention on reinforcing the positive changes and growth we achieve.

Look to yourself for progress.

The greatest thing
in the world is
to know how to
belong to oneself.

—Montaigne

Be Your Own Best Friend

A recovering addict I know had one relapse after another for months before he finally was able to surrender and accept his need. After one very discouraging slip, this man returned to a group meeting where he encountered several of his Twelve Step friends:

An oldtimer with years of sobriety nodded to him and asked "How's it going?"

"Terrible; just awful," the man responded. "I've been drinking again."

"Well," said the other man, "it could have been worse."

"Worse? How could it possibly be worse?"

"It could have been me," the oldtimer replied.

A selfish attitude? *I think not.* We must secure our own recovery before we can be helpful to others. We simply cannot give away something we don't yet have. Truly, we are custodians of our own recovery. Since our problems with addiction were self-induced, our potential for recovery in a Twelve Step Program depends to a great extent on how good we are to ourselves—in other word, how fair, and kind, and honest we are with ourselves. Even after acknowledging our addiction, some of us continued to treat ourselves with great disdain. Positive progress depended on our ability to begin making significant character changes.

"I'm my own worst enemy." Now that's a statement I'd guess all addicts think or say to themselves at some time. Once we begin to make some progress in recovery, one of our primary goals should be to reduce the incidence of regression or slips during our growth. It is quite common for some slips and regression to occur. Hopefully, these slips and regressions will be minor and brief.

There are times, however, when the most we can do is tread water as we try to hold our own in maintaining recovery and rebuilding self-worth. At these critical times in recovery, each of us must continue to contrast in our minds the people we used to be and the people we are now. We must remember that just as we're capable of being our own worst enemy… we're also capable of being our own best friend. Once we begin losing sight and appreciation of our success with sobriety, any relapse—even a spiritual or emotional "slip"—can lead to tremendous guilt. We must never forget the good things we've come to know in recovery. Self-forgiveness is strength, not weakness. If God has forgiven us, why can't we forgive ourselves?

The directions we take with both our progress and our regressions in recovery are issues of choice: We can like ourselves or hate ourselves; we can lift ourselves up or put ourselves down; we can be for ourselves or against ourselves; we can choose to be proud and happy or degraded and miserable. Our individual and/or collective actions, attitudes, and thoughts direct us toward one or the other of these choices. The negative approach almost always seems easier at first. When we are truly depressed, finding fault with ourselves is effortless. And, at those times, suffering doesn't require much effort either. In fact, there's a distinct danger of becoming so accustomed to hurting that we're unable to live comfortably unless we are feeling uncomfortable. It doesn't take long for negative thinking to take root and become a powerful habit in our lives.

The enemy within is a master at generating and justifying feelings of unworthiness. Our negative inner voice never tires of the lament that we are born losers, unable to get others to care about us...even with our best efforts.

The enemy within urges us to judge ourselves by what we are *not*. Acceptance of reality gives us an opportunity to stop mistreating ourselves and start changing in positive ways.

The enemy within prompts us to set impossible goals for ourselves that inevitably lead to failure. In time, the only outcome that makes an impression is failure. Many of us stopped trying entirely. We'd tell ourselves, "It's no use. Give up. You can't win, so why beat your head against a wall?"

The enemy within convinces us to take on the role of self-berater. When our thought processes are faulty, constant self-belittling eventually evolves in the mind as an act of virtue. Self-cruelty becomes a way of proving to ourselves that we *deserve* punishment; martyrdom is then only a step away.

Recovery helps us stop the cycle of mistreating ourselves. What transforms the enemy within to best-friend status? *Self-honesty.* Taking that very first step in a Twelve Step Program represents a great awakening. When we first admit that we are powerless over our addiction and that our lives have become unmanageable, we enter the world of honesty.

When we are entirely honest, we feel a relief that is similar to "getting the monkey off our backs." Taking that first step rids us of the need to lie and deceive others and ourselves. Gone are reasons to be deceitful, to seek alibis and excuses, and to look for loopholes in living. When we embrace reality, we see more clearly why honesty is so vital in our search for self-worth. We discover that we are honest not because honesty is expected of us, not because we are told we cannot find a new life unless we are honest, not even because we have been told that "honesty is the best policy." *We are honest because it makes us feel more completely ourselves.*

Learning to accept truths and facts with an open mind is another important part of the process of transforming our own worst enemy into our own best friend. We learn in our Twelve Step Program that when we say we cannot do something, we're actually assuring ourselves that we *won't* be able to do it.

We become our own best friend when we have confidence that we can rid ourselves of faulty thinking and compulsive behavior and become the best people we are capable of being. If we believe in our hearts that we can meet and exceed our own expectations, we will find the ability to do so. We become our own best friend when we concentrate on the triumphs of each day, rather than on the disasters of the past. We can start this process by recognizing how far we have come from the addiction that used to dominate our lives.

When we learn that we can be our own best friend, we become more comfortable with self-encouragement and self-praise. In fact, self-praise can be as simple as having confidence that we can be the best people we're capable of being. This conviction is invaluable to us as we rebuild self-worth. When we become self-praisers, we essentially break ties with the enemy within us. In abstinence, we dislike ourselves most when we are cruel to others. Enhanced self-worth helps us treat others more compassionately. We are well aware of the fact that those who find it impossible to love others are actually incapable of being kind to themselves. If all of this brings thoughts of selfishness, we perhaps should just substitute the word *self-care* for the word *selfish*. Good self-care leads naturally to caring for others. Concern for ourselves and concern for others work together to rebuild self-worth.

*P*ractice self-encouragement and self-praise at every opportunity.

Be Your Own Best Friend

The spirit of self-help is the root of all genuine growth in the individual...help from within invariably invigorates.

—Samuel Smiles

Give Yourself Credit

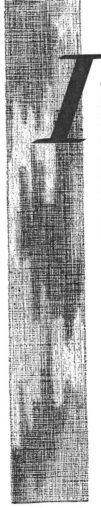

I once heard about a young, impatient newcomer to the Program who was unsure of his ability to cope on his own in recovery. He continued to cling to his dependency on people, places, and things. In fact, he was having great difficulty with the Program and ready to drop it altogether when he shared a suggestion with an oldtimer in his group: "I don't think our fellowship offers enough guidance," he said. "Newcomers should be provided with a simple, concise guide—a book of practical suggestions and tools for dealing with the problems we all encounter in recovery, a book with answers that can be readily understood." The oldtimer responded immediately: "I have just the book for you! And I'll bring it for you tomorrow. Meet me in the city park at noon."

At noon the next day, the oldtimer met the young man in the park. He promptly handed him the book he'd promised and said,

"Keep the cover of this book closed until you reach the bench at the top of that hill. Then, sit down and open it. In that book, you'll find the help you are seeking." The young man did as he was directed. When he turned back the large book cover, he stared intently at what was revealed inside—the source for all his solutions, as recommended by the oldtimer. The young man was startled, but he understood immediately. *Within the book was nothing but a mirror.*

Indeed, each person is the solution to his or her problems and/or blocks in recovery. We know that we cannot change other people, so we must accept the reality that no one else can change *us*. We can take direct action to solve problems that handicap us in recovery; we do this by utilizing the tools provided by the principles of the Twelve Step Program.

Change of character and change of attitude are the goals referred to when others tell us that "no one can do it *for* you." No one else can—or will—take credit for our progress. Oldtimers are being honest and helpful when they tell us that "the most we can do is advise and extend a helping hand; the ultimate decision and the hard work must come from you." Remember, any degree of progress we make toward character change and growth is the result of our own efforts.

Even with our belief in miracles and our commitment to positive action and thinking, we learn in recovery that we cannot passively depend on these things for our emotional growth. If we work the Twelve Step principles in our lives, it will be *impossible* for us not to change. But we must do the changing ourselves. And so, when change *does* occur in our lives, we should give ourselves credit for it. While we're aware that others have helped us immensely, we know that we must do what needs to be done *ourselves*. When we recognize and accept the credit we deserve for our efforts, we take important steps toward rebuilding our self-worth.

The steps of recovery programs are important, but so is the relatively short list of promises guaranteed by sobriety and found on page 84 of the *Big Book*. Among the changes promised those of us living the Twelve Steps: that we will change our attitude and outlook on life, that we will intuitively find solutions to problems that used to baffle us, and that we will no longer fear people or economic insecurity. These promises would surely fall into the category of *sheer fantasy* for recovering people were it not for the statement that follows them—that these seemingly extravagant promises *"will always materialize if we work for them."*

Our spiritual progress is not a gift, but a natural outcome of our efforts. Other people can show us the way to grow emotionally, but we must do the work ourselves. The "gifts" of recovery come to us only after we've undergone a spiritual experience or awakening. We are grateful for these miraculous turnabouts in thinking and behavior. But we learn early in recovery that we cannot depend on miracles and we cannot expect to have peace of mind for the rest of our lives…without continuing effort. Our ongoing task in recovery is one of developing perspective—of identifying, refining, and adopting values for living. But we also need to continue working on attitude changes in recovery—especially when we encounter emotional blocks or character defects.

The more effective we are in changing our character and attitudes, the greater our progress in rebuilding self-

Give Yourself Credit

worth. We must learn to be comfortable with the process of change in order to grow emotionally and spiritually. It's no easy task to make the emotional changes required to achieve and maintain sobriety. Each of us must find effective ways to make permanent changes in our lives on a daily basis. We also must give ourselves credit for finding creative, productive ways to stay healthy and clear in our thinking.

Some recovering people find it helpful to combine emotional tasks with physical tasks. Consider the experiences of a married couple, both recovering alcoholics. The man explains his situation this way:

"The most frustrating problem I have is with resentment, often called the *killer* of sobriety. I've discovered that it's not productive for me to confront the people I resent, because they're usually unaware that they displease me in the first place. So, I clear my mind and soul by taking my resentments to the woodpile behind the house. There's always a large quantity of wood chunks out there that must be chopped into proper size for firewood. For long periods of time I chop, making each blow a savage attack aimed at destroying an unhealthy attitude or resentment I have at that time. I always come away from this physically demanding task with a clearer, more peaceful mind...and a larger supply of useful firewood as well."

The woman describes her experience this way:

"During my daily inventories, I have difficulty focusing on character defects that must be removed. I find that I don't always want to let go of them. So each Saturday, I bake bread. The process requires a sustained effort of hard kneading. Each kneading motion I make is a blow at another defect. At the end of these bread-baking sessions, I feel great…and I have some tangible results as well."

We cannot successfully approach recovery in a timid way. Our acceptance includes admitting that our lives had become unmanageable. And with that admission comes a freedom from distraction in our approach to solutions. This new freedom is itself a valuable tool for rebuilding self-worth. We have only to make use of it and give ourselves credit for regaining it. It is only through work and action that we can achieve our full potential for self-worth. If we believe that we've been given a new life through abstinence, then the best (and probably only) way to honor that gift is to give of ourselves each day. The result will be increased self-confidence.

The more committed we are to continuing our work toward positive change, the more durable will be our feelings of adequacy and worth. If we lose our commitment and discontinue our work, we will eventually return to the sick thinking that dominated our days of addictive acting out—days when giving up appealed to us because it was clearly the easiest way out, the path of least resistance. As we work to rebuild self-worth, we must resist using strategies of denial or rationalization. When we persevere without playing destructive "games," we learn that adversity can be a blessing. The more time and energy we spend dodging adversity and opportunities to overcome it, the less confidence we'll have in ourselves. Feelings of inadequacy are bred by avoidance, denial, rationalization, and—of course—giving up.

That old suggestion to "let it all hang out" is a useful bit of advice as we work to rebuild self-worth. Indeed, it is difficult to envision the return of self-worth to anyone who is using precious time and energy to cover up character defects and problems. It often is said in programs of recovery that we are only as sick as our secrets. If we permit negative, unresolved thoughts and feelings to simmer within us, our attitudes will remain unhealthy and create pain for us. To achieve a healthier mind and outlook on life, we must rid ourselves of the sickness that prevents us from coping with adversity...and success. In other words, we must unload our emotional baggage before we can adequately attend to our recovery.

When we recovering people relapse into excessiveness, we usually experience agonizing guilt. We may even lose confidence that we're *capable* of returning to a solid recovery. It can be very easy to forget how well we were doing in recovery. We recovering addicts have many things in common with each other, including a tendency to shine a bright light on whatever we do that is wrong. So often, we emphasize our errors and small sins while deemphasizing our strengths and good deeds.

Serenity enters our lives when we are, with ample modesty, self-praisers. Self-encouragement can work many small miracles in our recovery from addiction. Self-praise can be an antidote to negative thinking. We must learn to give ourselves credit when we accomplish something. If we can benefit by admitting when we are wrong (and we can) we will also benefit by humbly taking credit when we are right. Expecting praise from others can be problematic—the time and energy used in waiting creates feelings of resentment and rejection. Besides that, praise from others is not as important as self-praise.

Compliments from others are short-lived, but the feelings associated with self-praise contribute to our sense of ongoing fulfillment and self-worth.

Gaining self-approval is a goal more worthy of our time and energy than gaining approval from others. We must be gentle with ourselves; we can learn to forgive ourselves as well as we forgive others. We must learn to be comfortable with feelings of pride and resist all efforts to be people-pleasers. With action, perseverance, confidence, patience, and dedication comes a feeling of worthiness that enables us to say, "I am, through my work and action in recovery, enjoying the best *now* and the best *me* of my life."

Make a habit of recalling the triumphs of each day—no matter how small—rather than dwelling on shortcomings, missteps, and mistakes.

Give Yourself Credit

What is our

praise or pride

But to imagine

excellence and

try to make it?

—Richard Purdy Wilbur

Take Another Look at Pride

Early in my own recovery, I heard a story about a young man with three years of sobriety who was selected to carry out an important writing assignment for his Twelve Step fellowship. He felt grateful and honored to have been chosen for the assignment; his background and experience were perfectly suited to the task. The young man carried out the task in a superb manner and everyone in the fellowship seemed pleased with his efforts.

But in the aftermath of his achievement, this young man realized that he was very uncomfortable with the sense of pride he felt. He subsequently sought advice from an oldtimer in his group saying, "I'm feeling proud of what I did and that worries me; I've learned that pride is a dirty word in recovery." Drawing on his many years of personal growth in recovery, the oldtimer responded in this way: "False, unjustified, ego-driven pride is bad, yes. But there's nothing wrong in feeling pride in something when you realize you did not accomplish it completely by yourself. The sharing and service that characterize recovery programs constantly remind us that nobody in our fellowship walks alone in any act of giving."

Like this young man, many of us wisely began to see pride as a primary character defect early in our recovery. Oldtimers in our Twelve Step groups warned us that pride was the shortcoming most likely to impede our progress toward serenity and long-term sobriety. Indeed, *false* pride stayed with many of us to the depths of our dependency, fueling our denial and resistance. Remember the words of "pride" we had for concerned people in our lives? *Don't push me. I'll handle my own problems. If I ever get bad enough, I'll just quit using…but I'll do it* my *way.* In those days, we desperately wanted to create the illusion for ourselves (and others) that we could continue to make our own choices, never understanding that we'd already squandered them. In recovery, we can be grateful that we did not cling to our pride—and the right to reject help—all the way to our death.

But despite our struggles with pride during our active addiction, there is a positive side to pride that makes it acceptable and useful to us in recovery. In fact, we must learn to have pride in our growth or we will obstruct the process of rebuilding self-worth. Pride assures us that we have the wisdom to rise above devastating character defects.

In recovery, we need not be fearful of pride— provided it is true pride, not false. Simply stated, false pride is pride that is dishonest, contrived, and/or used for rationalization or denial. False pride is damaging not so much because of how it makes us look to others, but in how it appears to us when we look inward.

True pride is essentially justified self-satisfaction. And this kind of pride relates to self-regard rather than to outward achievement or public acclaim. True pride usually is reflective in nature and it most often comes after an accomplishment resulting from careful analysis and hard work. What we might consider pride in our ability to accomplish something in the here and now is really confidence, the by-product of an earlier achievement. As is true with many other character assets required for success, pride in doing always follows—never precedes—a deed.

Another element of pride unique to those of us who maintain recovery from addiction: the realization that we did not achieve sobriety through our efforts alone. Those of us who win our battles with dependency always have had some help beyond our own bodies and souls. That help may have come in the form of assistance or encouragement from other people, from the precepts we have studied, and/or from our faith in a Higher Power. When we know that we never walk alone in any victory, then we know the kind of pride that reinforces self-worth.

There are many occasions in recovery when we feel pride in other people, particularly newcomers who succeed in turning their lives around. Most of us are quite willing to tell these people how proud we are of them. In turn, we are "rewarded" by the display of gratitude we see expressed in their faces. If we can rightfully be proud of others in recovery, why can't we be proud of ourselves?

True pride does not lead to an inflated ego, nor does it threaten the precious quality of our humility; true pride simply enhances our sense of self-worth. Regardless of how much our self-worth has been compromised by addiction, we're on track for rebuilding it when we take pride in our accomplishments in recovery and make this acknowledgment: that our accomplishments come from our practice of the principles introduced to us by other people in the recovery fellowship.

We can make a good start toward accepting positive, true pride in ourselves by thinking of our *acts*, rather than *ourselves*, as worthy of pride. Any deed we do can be a prideful one; it is the *act* that we are proud of. Justifiable pride seems easier to accept when we understand this concept. Even when we give credit for our successes entirely to God or our Higher Power, we can rightfully feel proud that we were entrusted to carry out an action willed for us, then given the necessary tools to carry it out.

True pride and feelings of self-worth grow naturally when we learn that we must make commitments and we must keep them. Those of us who have difficulty thinking of commitments as building blocks of self-worth may find it helpful to recall a pattern of behavior common in addiction: making commitments in order to avoid controversy or conflict without having the capacity, intention, or wherewithal to keep these commitments. In fact, during the height of our addiction, it seems that every promise we made was broken sooner or later. When we disregarded our promises to others, the only pride we felt was false pride in our arrogant belief that we had outwitted another "do-gooder" by appeasing him or her with empty promises. Most of us subsequently had regrets for failing to keep our promises, regrets that further undermined our self-worth.

Conversely, each time we follow through on a commitment we make, our self-worth is fortified. Of course, we need to begin with simple commitments. Then, as we successfully meet those commitments—however small—we move on to more complex ones. This progression from simple commitments to more complex ones represents growth; in fact, there is no description of growth that is more fundamental. Personal growth is most certainly an achievement worthy of pride.

It is helpful to remember that habits formed during years of faulty thinking and addictive behavior will be at least as difficult and time-consuming to disregard as they were to develop in the first place.

No one can make you

feel inferior without

your consent.

—Eleanor Roosevelt

_____

Confront Feelings of Inadequacy

or many of us, feelings of inferiority and a sense of somehow having been born "less than" others made our decline toward compulsion and addiction seem almost inescapable. It should not surprise us that these feelings follow us into a recovery program. But to progress in recovery, we must break free from feelings of inadequacy. Identifying and confronting these feelings will help us recognize them and ultimately eliminate them from our lives.

At one time or another, almost all addicted people feel "less than" others who have not been burdened with the "curse" of addiction. Unfortunately, these feelings of inferiority make it almost impossible for the addict to surrender to reality and reach out to others for help. During our active addiction, we struggled with many erroneous beliefs, including one that "the world" was constantly judging us and our behavior. To complicate

47

things, after years of *last binges*, we completely lost confidence in ourselves and our ability to change or take control of our lives. It seems that each time we failed in our attempts to straighten out our lives, we hated ourselves more. And that self-hatred only intensified when we saw how well other people lived their lives, without the added challenge of addiction.

Those of us who already felt "less than" others when we came to recovery were in for yet another blow. Remember, it is universally accepted that no addicted person can truly begin to recover until he or she surrenders to the reality of his or her condition and need. The very thought of this kind of surrender is devastating to someone who already feels inadequate in so many ways. Fortunately, surrender in a Twelve Step Program is a process that deflates false ego and grandiosity, exposes arrogant denial, and renders old ideas useless. It is true to say that surrender further undermines our self-esteem for a time *but* it also prepares us to ask for help. Recovery simply cannot take hold in our lives if we continue to believe that we are inferior and without value.

Given our compulsiveness, it was always difficult for us to be completely rational in our thinking. Conclusions about life patterns and priorities usually came slowly, sometimes painfully. But as excessive people, we were impatient and seldom satisfied with reality as we perceived it. Our history has been to look for the easy way out of pain, challenge, and uncertainty. And addictive substances and behaviors represented the perfect easy way out. No wonder, then, that those times when we *did* crash back to our real world, we felt inferior for having resorted to dishonesty in our efforts to appear to be like others.

48

But we never admitted our frustrations or our shame to others. We'd only strengthen our resolve that *nobody must ever know what I really am.* Then, we'd proceed to build more castles in the air, only to topple from them. Admitting our shams to others meant to us that we'd be playing directly into the hands of all those "enemies" who already judged us and disapproved. How we'd cringe at words we heard or attitudes we detected in the silent scorn and pity that were directed at us by folks we concluded were nothing but "smug busybodies."

Our low self-worth combined with feelings of anger when we saw judgment in the eyes of nonaddicts. For those of us who were chemically addicted, there was the added indignity of knowing, during brief times of sobriety, that family and friends were compensating for our "weaknesses," even enabling our addictive behavior by covering up for us or protecting us from natural consequences. Often, we were well aware of the fact that our loved ones were really shrouding our defects with secrecy so that the outside world wouldn't pity them for putting up with us. At times, we were filled with remorse for what we sensed we were doing to those we loved. We often came to the conclusion that those we were making so miserable with our behavior would actually *welcome* our death. We felt sure they were ashamed of us and that they actually would be better off without us. Such thoughts left their mark on our consciousness, even when we began a program of recovery.

Through all of our experiences with our addiction, we continued to be *all or nothing* people: If we couldn't have everything, we wanted nothing and we accepted our sense of being inferior. The erroneous thinking associated with addiction constantly reinforced our belief that we were somehow "less than" others. Even in recovery, we find that belief returning to haunt us from time to time. But if we allow feelings of inferiority to interfere with our progress, we limit our freedom of choice in recovery. Many of us came to recovery as experts on finding a quick, untimely, death; we need to replace this expertise with knowledge of how to *live*. Rebuilding something we thought we'd lost forever is a perfect beginning.

*B*elieve in yourself.

Confront Feelings of Inadequacy

Against the difference

in another person,

there is no other remedy

but love.

—Goethe

Acknowledge Your Need for Others

*T*here's a lovely analogy used in Twelve Step groups to illustrate the positive effects of sharing with others. Briefly, if goes something like this: People who truly share with others discover that the mirrored walls they had constructed to keep people out have become crystal-clear windows. When deep in addiction, these people saw only dismal reflections of themselves. But when these recovering addicts reach out and look beyond themselves, the clear glass they look through reveals to them a world of beauty filled with friends and fellowship. And then, these recovering people come to know that at last the world sees them as they always hoped they'd been seen by others.

During our days of active addiction, our denials were as much about denying our need for others as they were about denying our dependencies. It is helpful to remember that all wounds heal from the inside out; healing must start well below the surface. An important part of the healing process involves a shift from reliance on addictive substances and behaviors to a need for companionship. In recovery, we come to know that other people are not sources of our problems, but lifelines to solutions.

In recovery, we must learn to relate to people honestly. If we approach others in the Program in ways that are less than honest, we will be forced to resort to unhealthy people-pleasing to gain friendship and help. People-pleasing has no place in our efforts to rebuild self-worth because it is prompted and driven by the same character defect we must work to eliminate from our lives—*low self-worth*. People-pleasers know in their hearts that they're being dishonest. This dishonesty, in turn, produces guilt and shame and contributes to the sense that we are somehow "less than" others. We simply cannot rebuild self-worth when we know we are cheating to gain it.

There is a rewarding emotional process known as *mutuality* that characterizes the caring and sharing between people in Twelve Step groups. The word itself helps to illustrate the concept that we cannot give without receiving, nor can we receive without giving. Mutuality comes naturally in the early stages of recovery. Newcomers to a sharing program are usually delighted to discover that fellowship with others is important to their success in the Program and that oldtimers in the Program need newcomers in order to maintain what they've already achieved in recovery.

If we're concerned that we are not utilizing mutuality in our sharing with others, we need to remember that each person participating in a recovery program begins by identifying his or her addiction. When we make this acknowledgment in the presence of others, we place ourselves in the company of everyone else present. After that, each word we utter in our Twelve Step fellowship represents another fresh start in regaining self-worth. We will know that mutuality is working for us when we are able to identify with others in the process of sharing problems.

When we were in our active addiction, we almost always resented people who attempted to reach out to us. Some of us even lost respect for those who, time after time, extended a helping hand to rescue us. Some of us even questioned the sanity of those who persisted in trying to help us. We couldn't imagine anyone in his or her right mind not seeing that we were hopeless.

In recovery, we grow through the mutuality of human exchange. For example, when we offer someone a genuine compliment, we also strengthen our own sense of self-worth. When we make a conscious effort to approach a fellow recovering addict and offer sincere praise regarding his or her progress, we are rewarded by an "outer show of an inner glow" from that person. It is then we know that our recognition of another person's achievement has helped that person mark his or her own progress. We will feel a healthy, genuine pride when we know that we have helped another recovering person rebuild his or her own self-worth. And we will have gratitude when praise from others comes our way as well. This mutuality creates a subtle but positive sense in us that "if that other person is making progress that I can notice, then I am probably growing in ways that others are aware of as well." At this point, we realize the power of

Acknowledge Your Need for Others

positive relationships and how far we have come from the "nobodies" we thought ourselves to be when we were overwhelmed by our active addiction.

When we actively look for the good in others and tolerate the bad that we find, we are holding up a mirror called *self-worth* for ourselves to study. When we are open enough to be inspired by the success of others and taught by their mistakes, we are reassuring ourselves of our worth in the face of both success and failure. And the applause we give to others does much more than make us feel good. Sharing with others is not an automatic act. We will experience no real reward for giving away something of ourselves that we don't want or have no further use for. We must give to others the qualities of ourselves that we truly want and need, things we cherish and use. Our genuine sharing with others assures us that we will never lose these qualities completely; these qualities will leave their goodness within us while showing up in the emotions of others.

When we reach out to others in recovery, we also gain a new understanding of forgiveness. We must learn to relate to those we seek to forgive. We need to make an effort to understand how others harmed or misused us or if we have somehow misinterpreted their actions or comments. This approach to forgiveness applies to others as well as ourselves. With this attitude to help us, we may find that we have less trouble than we anticipated in forgiving ourselves for our *own* errors. We may also see how much effort and time we wasted with our anger and how we can avoid such traps in the future. These new insights will contribute in a positive way to our feelings of self-worth.

The more we relate to others in positive ways, the better we'll understand the adage that nothing worth doing should be done alone. This concept helps reinforce our sense of worth in our exchanges with others. Instead, we will be empowered to say, "I am special because I *choose* to accept help from those who taught me how to grow spiritually." Positive relationships with people will also help us believe that we are loved and wished well by others. And there is no greater love than wishing someone well.

Most of us failed to realize during our active addiction that when we were lonely, it was because our feelings of low self-worth were serving to isolate us from others. Our overwhelming feelings of being inadequate and unworthy forced us to draw away from people and wrap ourselves in a blanket of isolation. But when we nurture a belief in ourselves in recovery, we begin to emerge from our shell of loneliness and boredom.

It is important to realize that we need other people not only because we share similar problems, but because of our differences. Indeed, our collective strength lies in our differences. As we seek ways to work out our problems, we are encouraged to share *because* of the differences that exist between us. It is because of our differences that we must engage in giving and receiving, caring and sharing, love and service. Twelve Step recovery programs certainly accept and welcome differences, but they also value diversity. Without the opportunity to learn from different people, our viewpoints and values will be narrow in scope and less useful to us in recovery.

It doesn't take much time in the Program to realize that if we slip back into addictive behavior, our lives will surely

Acknowledge Your Need for Others

get worse instead of better. We need to create a confidence in each abstinent today. Confidence is needed to keep us assured that all is well today and will continue to be, just as long as we continue to do the proper groundwork. If we nurture our confidence, tomorrow will be in good hands. The confidence of abstinence is a fearless trust and a blind faith. We need to have a combination of optimism and realism about the fullness of our capabilities and the extent of our limitations.

Emotional growth will proceed only if we have confidence that we are not fundamentally weak-willed or cowardly. We must develop the belief that we are people of courage. Some of us accept things readily and with comparative ease; others of us fight any kind of surrender for a long period of time, perhaps through several relapses. But we are truly courageous when we can acknowledge and confront our addiction. Make no mistake, it takes fortitude, confidence, and persistence to battle addiction.

As we work to build our confidence and courage, it's best to focus on action. If we wait for a set of rules to emerge before we take action, it may be too late. Will power and high intelligence won't solve our problems. We must learn to trust our instincts, our emotions, and the concepts for living we have developed based on the principles of the Twelve Steps. But we won't go far in recovery with only abstinence and feelings of self-satisfaction. Feeling content with those things can lead to complacency. And complacency can lead to this kind of thinking: "I'm too busy doing bigger things to stay involved in my Program" or "I'm clean and sober. What more can I want or do?" But abstinence isn't all there is. Abstinence alone is not enough to fill out and balance our lives. True, ongoing abstinence is a fundamental goal in recovery, but it is not the *only* goal. Another critical goal is ongoing spiritual and emotional growth.

In our Twelve Step Program, we learn that we can only serve well in helping others when we give to the best of our ability. When we love unselfishly without seeking love in return, what we give away is our greatest reward. We learn in our Twelve Step group that the more we receive the more we need to give, and the more we give away, the more we get back in return. Willingness must motivate our sharing. Sharing is leaving behind something of spiritual value following an exchange with someone. Those who truly share with others develop enduring instincts to *be* friends rather than *make* friends.

Cultivate the ability to relate to others with honesty and care.

The life which is
unexamined is not
worth living.

—Plato

Develop Skills for Self-Evaluation

ecently, a Twelve Step group member told me what she believes is the greatest benefit of her recovery: that while her Program never dictates where she should go, it does keep her informed of just where she is in her emotional and spiritual progress. Here's what she said: "I cannot be faithful to my potential or my goals unless I pause frequently and determine where my progress has placed me on any given day. It's like being the captain of a ship at sea. Even though the captain has traveled a certain route hundreds of times, he still depends, each day, on a navigator to inform him just where the ship is on the ocean's great expanse. I'm grateful that I have access to measuring guides along the course of my recovery— other people in the Program and my inventories and daily self-evaluation."

Utilize, don't analyze—during our first days and weeks in a recovery Program, that was helpful advice frequently shared with us by oldtimers. Then, our primary concern was the intense struggle with addictive substances and compulsive behavior. At that time, it was quite appropriate to take the advice of others literally and practice the Program without giving much thought to why and how it worked. Indeed, during our first efforts to achieve abstinence, simple utilization of the Program, *without analysis,* proved to be the most useful strategy.

But when the immaturity of addiction gives way to the mature reasoning of a balanced recovery, we are well advised to reconsider the "utilize don't analyze" warning. In fact, recovery from addictive living gradually moves us from a basic program of "do and don't" instructions to a comprehensive program for achieving and maintaining a full and balanced lifestyle.

We cannot live full and balanced lives in abstinence unless we learn more about our own productive thinking and behavior. And until we begin to analyze and evaluate our own thinking and behavior in recovery, we cannot make meaningful progress in rebuilding self-worth.

Peace of mind in recovery comes when we eliminate and/or effectively manage defects that we have identified as detrimental to our spiritual growth. Self-satisfaction and pride result from making amends to others. But neither of these things can be accomplished without self-evaluation.

We perhaps need to remind ourselves that self-evaluation is of little value to us if it focuses only on our liabilities; assets are far more important to us in the process of rebuilding self-worth. When we dwell on our shortcomings, we only reinforce negative thinking. It was the focus on our character defects that undermined our self-worth in the first place. We need to actively work to eliminate faults from our lives rather than ruminating about them. Recognizing ways to utilize neglected good qualities in our recovery will build reserves of self-confidence.

Simply by maintaining abstinence, we have come such a long way from being the "less than" people we thought ourselves to be during our active addiction. It is unfortunate but true that only a very small percentage of people who struggle with addiction eventually find and maintain sobriety. Keeping this fact in mind, we can justifiably come to this conclusion: "I *am* special. Through my efforts and the help of others who know how to guide me, I have found a second chance at a full and satisfying life." If we can truthfully say this, how can we possibly continue to abuse ourselves with thoughts that we are somehow inferior to other people?

We will develop respect for our assets, gifts, and talents only when we thoroughly examine the quality of emotions within us such as honesty, gratitude, and humility.

Honesty, the key to so many positive changes in recovery, is also important to finding our true selves and measuring our progress. Most of us learned so much about honesty in that moment when we first admitted we were addicted and had completely lost all freedom of choice in our behavior. Each step we've taken toward serenity and security since that time has depended upon honesty. *People who are honest with themselves can see the way to self-worth.*

Evaluating our thoughts and behavior with a clear and free mind can reveal new purpose in life for us as

Develop Skills for Self-Evaluation

recovering people. Our self-worth is positively affected when we realize two things: that our compulsiveness hid our motivation and sense of direction for ourselves and that, as recovering people, we are among the relative few who've managed to clear away the hindrances of addiction.

During our active addiction, we'd moan "why me?" about the sorrows and pains that came to us, making us feel even more unworthy and incapable. But in recovery, we can joyously exclaim "why me?" about the fortunate and beautiful things we experience. In recovery, we can count among our many blessings an awareness of deep gratitude. Feelings of gratitude serve as a protection against self-pity. When self-pity was our game, we'd complain (or think to ourselves), "Why can't I have fun doing exactly as I want to do—like other people?"

But with a growing sense of gratitude, we're be more likely to say, "Why am I no longer possessed with compulsions? Why am I among the lucky ones who don't have to go through all that again?" And we may also ask, "Why is the ailment that I have one that can be arrested for life if I simply resist—one day at a time—thinking and behaving in a way that was completely destroying my life?" We can remind ourselves that so many diseases require years of medication and treatment. As addicts, we had only to pick up a telephone and attend a meeting to find help that transformed our lives—caring people who knew exactly how we felt because they'd had similar experiences. How relatively easy it was for us to get help. Why were we so blessed? With gratitude, we also ask, "Why was I chosen to find a recovery program that has brought me new purpose in life and included me in a wonderful fellowship of people who desperately need other people—and now know where to find them?"

Rebuilding Self-Worth in Recovery

People in recovery need to ask themselves the foregoing questions each time the cunning, baffling, powerful, jealous, and tenacious disease of addiction threatens to entice them back into "stinkin' thinkin.'"

Along with gratitude comes humility. Humility is an asset we must not try to force upon ourselves; the result will be a false humility that will be harmful to ourselves and to others as well. If our minds are open to receive, we will discover that humility can be as simple as being willing to learn. Humility is one of the best tools available for growth. In the process of self-evaluation, we ask ourselves how humble we are. As we analyze our thoughts and behaviors, it won't take long for us to become aware of the fact that honesty and humility are closely connected. Working together, honesty and humility increase our willingness and openness. So then, instead of trying to use false pride as a weapon, we learn to recognize and cope with *truth*. As a result, self-worth conquers unhealthy pride.

Humility will ease the tough task of saying "I'm sorry." But if we approach that act with remembrances of past *humiliation* foremost in our minds, our progress in building self-esteem will be impeded. We will feel better about ourselves when we learn that no apology ever need be a sign of humiliation. To admit that we were wrong when that is the truth can be an example of the maturity that is the byproduct of enhanced self-worth. It is natural for us to take pride in our character growth when it is manifested by the knowledge that no apology or amends we make are meaningful when we feel shame. Humility makes apology with dignity possible.

Some of our feelings of being inferior came from being hurt by the words or actions of others, or from being

Develop Skills for Self-Evaluation

completely ignored by others. Truly humble people suffer fewer rebuffs from others because they have learned to *live* with people, rather than manipulate or misuse them. We need other people! There is perhaps no greater expression of true humility than the words *We can do what I can't.*

*R*emember that self-evaluation is not a one-time project, but an ongoing assignment. Daily self-evaluation is essentially a periodic "visit" to oneself.

Be wise today;

'tis madness to defer.

—Edward Young

Practice the HOW of Recovery...Today

*T*here was a medical doctor, renowned for his research skills, who achieved a period of recovery in a Twelve Step group. After a year in the Program, however, this doctor concluded that he'd learned enough to sustain his own recovery. He decided to leave the Program and instead "serve" the addicts of the world by conducting research on various approaches to recovery. He subsequently put together a rather elaborate strategy, established "measurable" goals, and began his experimentation—on himself. Eventually, this doctor landed in a hospital bed—his own recovery in shambles, his research incomplete. One day, a woman from his Twelve Step group came to visit him in the hospital after not seeing him for well over a year. Inveterate researcher that he was, the doctor decided to continue on from his hospital bed. "Tell me, Mary," he asked, "how do you work *your* Program?" Mary's reply came unhesitatingly and in a single word: *"Simply."*

Keep it simple is surely an important concept to remember as we work to make recovery an integral part of our daily lives. One way of keeping the Twelve Step Program simple and accessible to us each day is to remember and practice what some refer to as the HOW of recovery: *H*onesty—*O*pen-mindedness—*W*illingness.

Honesty is fundamental to sustained recovery. We simply cannot progress unless we are "rigorously" honest with ourselves. It is impossible to grow spiritually and emotionally if we say one thing yet do and/or think something different. We will not develop real respect for ourselves until we "walk the talk"—in other words, until there is congruence between what we say and what we think and do in recovery.

Honesty can be habit-forming in recovery, just as dishonesty was habit-forming during our active addiction. We'll actually develop an affinity for honesty if we concentrate on it in our search for self-worth. When we experience honesty working for us in positive ways, it reinforces our sense of its value in our lives. In time, we will practice honesty simply because it feels right and fortifies our self-worth.

Open-mindedness is another element vital to ongoing recovery. Open-mindedness reminds us that self-worth is a byproduct of both giving and receiving. Open-minded people respect the rights of others to have opinions differing from their own. An open mind thrives on new ideas and therefore cultivates new relationships. When we are open to the experiences and ideas of others, we are less likely to struggle with resentments, envy, and jealousy—all blocks to the development of self-esteem.

When we're open-minded, we improve our ability to utilize the positive elements we find in the different opinions we encounter. We will learn to respect our growing ability to *disagree without being disagreeable*. We also make good progress toward self-worth when we learn to tolerate the closed minds we find along the way—and benefit from the dangers we see in those attitudes.

Open-mindedness also motivates us to take the kind of positive action that leads to enhanced self-worth. We must never lose sight of the fact that when we lock the doors of our minds, we keep out of our hearts more of value than can ever be protected by a closed mind. Tolerance of people, places, and situations clears the way for the action necessary to grow. The outlets for "working at recovery" are found in fellowships where recovering addicts combine their efforts to benefit all.

Open-mindedness leads naturally to another important asset for growth: good listening skills. During our active addiction, our denial was fueled and intensified by the blocks we set up in order to avoid discussion about our addictions and obsessions. In recovery, we need to remain open to discuss both problems and solutions with others. Another important consideration—attentive listeners seldom have time or reason to feel lonely, bored, or useless.

Willingness is another essential factor in sustained recovery. Willingness suggests an eagerness to learn and the openness to approach even that which is totally unfamiliar—so long as there is the possibility of a productive result. Willingness embraces readiness, the fact and feeling of preparedness to cope with whatever is encountered.

We can use our willingness to reach for new self-worth as long as we do not confuse it with willfulness. We must work on our ability to willingly accept reality and admit our limitations. We must also guard against confusion between willingness and will power. In fact, an unrestrained strong will can shut the door of the mind so tightly that only unrelenting willingness can reopen it. Willingness can rid us of fears while willfulness can lead us right back to our former belief that we were somehow born "less than" others. When we have a healthy sense of self-worth, our willingness will help us transform thoughts into realities.

Another important aspect of rebuilding self-worth lies in our awareness and acceptance that willingness points us in the direction of proper choices. Proper choices, in turn, lead us toward that time when we can say on this day and on any tomorrow, "*I am truly a worthy person, and for this I am humbly and honestly grateful.*"

For us addicted people, learning to live each day as it comes represents an almost revolutionary behavior reversal. After all, we're the same people who used to spend so much of our time regretting our sad pasts and fearing futures we felt sure would be dismal. In terms of solutions to problems, looking to the past may lead us to answers that are outmoded; looking to the future for answers is wishful thinking. To grow spiritually, we must live in the *now*. A day-by-day growing process has patience and persistence as its best assets. These assets cannot be replaced by anything else—not talent, nor genius, nor education. Our self-worth will increase if we learn to avoid the word "should." "Should" is an indefinite put-off-until-tomorrow word that really gets us nowhere in terms of motivation or action. Truly, this word *invites* rationalization. We will feel better if we substitute the word "will." Substituting "I *will* do" for "I *should* do" can make a subtle but powerful difference in our daily lives.

We begin making dramatic changes in our lives when we concentrate on life as it is *today*. Living in the present allows much less room for guilt or fear. Guilt materializes from errant yesterdays; fear arises from our worry about unknown tomorrows. Resentments develop from what already has been felt; anxiety develops from experiences yet to be confronted. When we can believe in our hearts that no wreckage of the future can ever be as devastating as the past we were strong enough to emerge from, we will find even more reason to believe in ourselves and our worth.

Resist temptations to project, procrastinate, or complicate.

I know of no more
encouraging fact than
the unquestionable
ability of man to
elevate his life by a
conscious endeavor.

—Henry David Thoreau

Raise Your Standards

*W*hen I stumbled into my first Twelve Step meeting, I had no expectation—or even hope—of achieving any kind of emotional or spiritual growth. My only goal, at the age of seventy, was to stop drinking, so that when I died, I'd leave this world as a sober person and not embarrass my family. But now, I'm amazed that my twenty years of recovery in a Twelve Step Program have resulted in more emotional and spiritual growth than the preceding seven decades of my life combined. And I can see now that my own growth is the direct result of continually setting new goals and working to achieve them.

One worthwhile goal in recovery is to be able to make the following statement: "Today, because I abstain, I'm the best me I've ever been." The chief benefit of this open-ended assessment is that it can be adjusted upward as we grow emotionally in recovery. In this way, the process of rebuilding self-worth never seems boring or hopeless.

By stating the fact that "I believe I am the best me ever," we challenge ourselves to make each day of our lives even better than the day before. Hence, we cannot relax and spend our time merely savoring the serenity, honesty, willingness, and tolerance we've found in recovery. Fortunately, we can transfer our dependency on substances and/or certain behaviors to a healthy, human need for friends and personal sharing. Recovery helps us understand that we grow emotionally when we share our experiences, strengths, and hopes with others who are working toward similar goals.

When our lives were in bondage to the power of our addiction, we conned ourselves into seeing hope for a brighter future by settling for just being "almost good enough" each day that we lived. Despite our daily resolve that "today will be different," all of our days ended in failure with our minds in a state of chaos. Our only comfort then was the vague sense that we "almost" spent a whole day without giving in to our addiction.

But in abstinence, "almost victories" are not victories at all. In order to rebuild self-worth, we need to understand that even a near-miss is a failure for people who are addicted. When we were in our active addiction, our disordered thinking convinced us that merely coming close was good enough. We now know that this belief system aided and abetted the progression of our disease.

As recovering people, we are aware that the chief hazard associated with accepting "almost victories" is the development of false pride. We usually explained our missed goals by blaming bad luck and the actions or inactions of others. We will progress in rebuilding self-worth if we truly believe this: when we resort to denying our responsibilities, we enable our sick egos to become sicker and more pervasive.

In recovery, we also learn that "almost" successes prevent us from attaining the self-worth we hope to achieve. How do we put a stop to these "almost" achievements? By knowing—through experience—our personal limitations and capabilities, and by setting goals that are realistic for us. When we have this knowledge and use it as well, we have a better chance of achieving our goals and developing sustained confidence in ourselves. These achievements, in turn, help us take yet another productive but reasonable step toward renewed self-worth. By taking ourselves out of the ranks of the "almost" people, we fortify ourselves against settling for half-measures or looking for answers in old ideas.

There is no disgrace in falling short of ambitious goals, but we need to recognize when and where our goals need adjustment. We will, however, have problems in recovery if we feel content even when we *consistently* fall short of our goals. If we're satisfied while repeatedly missing our goals, we might not even make the effort to adjust our scale for success. We are failures only if we fail to use our talents. The more effort we put into being the people we want to be, the better use we will make of our emerging confidence and self-worth. Our addiction forced us to continually say, "I'm no good; I'll never find recovery." Recovery replaces this attitude with confidence in our capabilities, our potentials, and our limitations. Simply stated, our self-esteem grows as our goals are adjusted upward. It is frequently said that there are few failures in a recovery program, but many quitters.

Raise Your Standards

Recovery is always a matter of choice. Every person, at any given moment in his or her life, is the result of the choices he or she has made. Dropouts from Twelve Step Programs are usually those people who want everything good to come to them without giving in return or even seeking ways of bringing permanent, positive change into their lives.

One newcomer to a Twelve Step group was ready to drop out when he mentioned during his group meeting that he was impatient about the future and wondered when his "ship" would come in—he spent much of his time in recovery wondering when his fortunes would change in a positive way. This man felt that he was doing what was required of him by attending Twelve Step meetings...and passively but not so patiently waiting for his life to be transformed. Then, one day, a wise oldtimer in his Twelve Step group informed him bluntly that "nobody ever finds a ship coming in unless he or she has sent out a ship or two in quest of treasures. When was the last time you sent out such a ship?"

Finding self-worth, like finding serenity, need not be treacherous or painful. We can even make a game of it. We are all familiar with the challenge of playing a game. We play games for enjoyment and recreation, or they really aren't worth playing at all. Yet, we play to win. We've all heard variations of the motto "It's not whether you win or lose, but how you play the game that counts." While that sentiment sounds good and offers helpful perspective, oftentimes it isn't satisfactory to us as competitive human beings. And when we're engaged in a contest with compulsion, we must win in order to continue our progress in recovery. We follow rules, as in all games. There can be no cheating. In abstinence, there

Rebuilding Self-Worth in Recovery

is one rule that comes before all others: it is the same as the name of the game of sobriety—*we don't use and/or engage in addictive behaviors.*

There are, however, some "mind games" we must discard in order to raise our standards in setting and achieving goals—rationalizations and denials that we enjoyed and employed during our years of addiction and compulsion—back then, when we were "almost winners."

Enhanced self-worth becomes more possible when we accept the fact that each person must cope with his or her own problems and also permit others to cope with their own problems. Going beyond any near-miss with renewed, dedicated effort must be—like most things in recovery—an "inside" job for each of us.

We will never make significant progress in rebuilding self-worth if we continue to cling to self-pity. After all, it was self-pity that made us believe that the only person with problems is the addicted person. Accepting the truth that *all* people have problems helps us learn to cope with adversity. And, coping with adversity helps us earn the right to consider ourselves "the best me" on any given day.

We cannot rebuild self-worth by trying to rid ourselves of emotions. We *need* emotions, they supply us with energy. All emotions contain great power, whether that power is positive or negative. As our confidence grows in recovery, we make choices about how we will use our emotions most productively.

For example, there is nothing wrong with anger…when it is directed at things that block or harm our progress in recovery. Anger can serve a useful purpose in character growth if we bring it out into the open and talk about it when it first evidences itself. We should not criticize another person's admission of his or her anger. When we hear a person in recovery admit to anger, we are wrong to assume that he or she is headed for a slip. Actually, that person venting his or her anger might be saving himself or herself from a slip by *disclosing* hurt and pain, rather than stuffing it inside.

Even after addicted people find sobriety in a Twelve Step Program, they still have a tendency to want all good things immediately. In their own way. On their own terms. But there's a basic conflict here because in addiction, most of us have become very skillful procrastinators.

We must guard against taking refuge in procrastination. We can reduce the urge to procrastinate by becoming involved in our recovery program and by personally taking care of problems when they first arise. We need to seek solutions actively; we must learn not to fear solutions. Action is the enemy of procrastination and a key to our continuing growth. One form of procrastination can be particularly disastrous to us as recovering addicts: putting off the action of sharing our problems and concerns with others. Many people delay opening up for fear of being criticized or ridiculed. Remember that our fellow members in Twelve Step groups give us the right to be wrong—and to be right.

One of the rewards of rebuilding self-worth can be found in nature's most interesting mirrors—the eyes of other people. Those of us who once wallowed in feelings of shame, regret, and remorse are inspired when we see a reflected image of our own achievements in the faces of those who loved and supported us during our addiction and our early, fragile stages of recovery.

Remember that nothing takes the place of persistence and the willingness to "press on" when faced with problems or challenges.

God, give use the grace
to accept with serenity
the things that cannot
be changed, courage to
change the things
which should be
changed, and the
wisdom to distinguish
the one from the other.

—Reinhold Niebuhr

Savor Change

*U*nless we are vigilant and treat ourselves with care and kindness, we will have difficulty overcoming five powerful blocks to the growth of self-worth: shyness, hesitation, timidity, doubt, and anxiety.

We can prevent these things from undermining our efforts in recovery if we develop zest and gusto as we work the Program. These words aren't used too much these days, but I maintain that they represent the spirit with which we must embrace and savor the change that recovery brings to our lives. In fact, I'd add another "old-fashioned" word to the formula for success: grit.

When I use the word zest, I'm thinking in terms of vitality, vigor, and dynamic involvement, along with the basic enjoyment of doing. Gusto is a spirited enthusiasm that helps us carry our positive sense of ourselves will beyond the "high" of a temporary achievement. Grit, as I see it, is an essential part of courage and fortitude; grit suggests the power of being resolute and tenacious in our efforts to rebuild self-worth. Combine these qualities with basic courage—the willingness to try to achieve something we once believed was far beyond our reach—and we're well on our way to maximizing positive change in our lives. But self-worth cannot be gulped down as rapidly as we develop it. We need to think in terms of savoring our newfound worth one "sip" at a time.

Whenever the old feelings of inadequacy begin to affect our thinking again, we need to remind ourselves just how far we've already come in our efforts to recover and rebuild self-worth. Feelings of being "less than" others must be quickly identified and countered with positive, self-affirming beliefs, thoughts, and actions. Without this balance, our self-judgment will quickly shift to the negative again. Our escape from compulsions and dependencies effectively teaches us that we never received any satisfaction whatsoever from our feelings of inferiority. We despised the thought that we were losers. Now, as we make or renew our commitment to rebuild self-worth, we have many opportunities to confront and win our battles with negative thinking.

Change motivated by fear is doomed to failure. If we are fearful, we will naturally be on the defensive and tend to relate to Satchel Paige's caveat: "Don't look back. Something may be gaining on you." When fear moves to the forefront of our thoughts, we need to take action to do whatever will keep us occupied with our spiritual growth. One of the antidotes for fear is introspection—contemplating choices that will be consistent with our growing sense of self-worth. We leave fear behind when we actively move toward a positive goal rather than running away in fear. Contemplation will bring answers as to the action that will be most constructive. We wait for proper answers to be formulated in our minds, knowing that snap judgments and impulsive actions may cause irreparable damage. And we make contact with others who are seeking advice and assurances. We respect our intuition, for it has grown out of experience. But we must not overlook the importance of faith and hope.

If we should get depressed in our efforts to rebuild self-worth (and we will), we first must remember that we are not alone. Depressions come to everyone at some time. Almost always, we will emerge from our temporary "down" feelings if we do not allow them to overtake our thinking and deplete our energy. Our growing sense of self-worth can ease us though minor crises by serving as a reminder that we are not inadequate. We can prevent a state of immobilization by telling ourselves that we are not being rejected by others—but by ourselves. The power of positive self-talk is essential as we seek to restore our balance in down times.

We relate and identify in patterns of change and growth with others who share our problems. In recovery, we feel no less than anyone else. Our adequacies match those of friends in fellowship who work with us toward peace of mind. Our capabilities and limitations compare with all who strive for self-worth. But while we share standards with many others in recovery, we are unique. With truth and love, we must find ways to remind ourselves of (and truly enjoy) our uniqueness and our worth. Remember that love without truth is sentimentality; truth without love is cruelty. And both sentimentality and cruelty are blocks to self-worth.

Self-worth leads to the very thing we once resisted so stubbornly—self-love. And when we love ourselves, we know who we are, what we need to do to please ourselves, and how we can set an example for others to follow. Being good to ourselves is not a form of selfishness or self-centeredness; being good to ourselves is one way to bolster a sagging ego that our previous feelings of inferiority turned into a downward-spiraling, energy-depleting state of mind.

*B*egin the quest for self-worth with determination
and continue it with patience.

Savor Change

As he thinketh in his heart, so is he.

—Proverbs 23:7

Renew Your Belief in Miracles

I remember hearing about a newcomer to a Twelve Step group who had a really engaging story to tell about how he happened to attend his first Twelve Step meeting. As he told this story to his group, he rattled off a number of rather remarkable coincidences that seemingly brought him to just the right place at just the right time to get the help he needed. After hearing his story, a woman in his group came over to him and said, "I think that you need to examine your belief that coincidence brought you to recovery. What you're identifying as coincidence is actually a series of miracles for which God chooses to remain anonymous."

Indeed, miracles and recovery are practically synonymous. An addicted person's first major miracle takes place when he or she, through abstinence, reenters conscious life from an existence of helplessness that is devoid of choices, freedom, and hope.

It is certainly true that abstinence must come first in recovery. Change and growth simply cannot take place until we are free from addiction. But abstinence is only the beginning of spiritual growth in recovery...as we are frequently reminded in our Twelve Step groups. People who see abstinence as their only goal in recovery will soon be wondering, as the song asks, "Is That All There Is?" Abstinence alone will never be enough. In order to transform our lives from active addicts to stable, recovering people who are free of obsessions and compulsions, we must continue to seek altered attitudes and spiritual growth.

We see other miracles take place in a caring and sharing program of recovery; these miracles don't just happen to a chosen few at rare moments, but all the time, to all former addicts who continue to seek spiritual growth in recovery. Each of us is given a new life in recovery, along with something addiction stole from us: *a purpose in life, a reason for living.*

Regardless of how long we've been in recovery, a series of miracles has already brought us a great distance from addiction. When we hit bottom with our addictions, we lost all hope for ourselves. Whatever self-esteem we'd had disappeared along with our ambitions, dreams, and desires. When we were in the depths of self-hate, we felt so unworthy it seemed hopeless to ask for help at all. Many of us remember sobbing to ourselves or others, "Who'd want to waste time on a failure—a nothing—like me?" This "I'm not worth helping" belief evolved from our disintegrating self-worth and led to our rejection of whatever success we *did* experience. We held the belief that we did not deserve to win or succeed at *anything...* including recovery.

When we were in our active addiction, we had no freedom of choice. We were slaves to our compulsions and obsessions; that is the nature of addiction. It is worthwhile to remember that we did not simply give up our addiction; we managed to escape from its fierce grip. At that point, our lives began anew. But even with the positive life changes that come to us in recovery, old ideas—particularly the harmful ones—are extremely difficult to shake. In recovery, we must learn to replace harmful ideas with helpful, positive ideas. On a daily basis, we need to substitute positive thinking for negative thir king. Healthy habits must be developed to replace the habits that got us into trouble in the first place. One of the most insidious habits we must free ourselves from in recovery is negative self-talk that tells us we're still somehow *less than* other people. The truth is this: in recovery, we have the same opportunities to find serenity and security in our lives as the least addicted people on earth. When we understand and accept this truth, we come to see it as a gift, the ongoing miracle that is recovery.

As we recover and grow spiritually, it is vitally important that we feel self-worth in our hearts. This important grounding provides us with the capacity to give of ourselves to others, freely and genuinely. Each day in recovery, we have life-enhancing opportunities to pass on our experiences, strengths, and hopes to others. This important sharing process brings purpose and shape to our lives, an overriding reason for living that can never be belittled or destroyed. The self-worth that evolves from helping another person without expecting a reward or return gesture leads to spiritual growth.

Even with miracles all around us in recovery, we must be patient as we work at rebuilding our self-worth. We must also learn to be satisfied with slow but steady change and growth in character. It helps to keep in mind the fact that growth—like life itself—is a continuing process, not a spectacular, one-time injection of fulfillment. For most of us, the growth process is likely to be a lifelong task of putting together all the best things for a rewarding existence and developing personal strengths and attributes that will satisfy us and serve us well.

We are among the most fortunate people on earth if we can embrace life as an interesting and stimulating process. When we see life as a process, we are much less likely to struggle with loneliness, boredom, or feelings of unworthiness. When we begin to realize that we can actually change our attitudes in recovery, we become aware of the ongoing miracle of recovery that nurtures self-worth and spiritual growth.

*C*herish the process of recovery, for it is truly a miracle unfolding.

Renew Your Belief in Miracles

*T*he miracle of recovery continues…and the miracle helps us as we work to regain precious human assets we thought we'd lost forever to our addiction. Self-worth is so critical to our sustained recovery. If we are to progress in our emotional and spiritual growth, we must continue to give special attention to self-care and our deepest feelings about ourselves.

Already, we've come such a long way… from our addiction, to our surrender, and through the difficult early stages of recovery. Now, our work in recovery focuses on growth that can be a source of renewal for the rest of our lives. As self-worth returns to balance and enhance your life, may it create for you a lifetime of *new mornings* and *second dreams*:

> *New Mornings* —each day, a fresh new opportunity to be "never better."

Second Dreams—fondest hopes and wishes forged and energized by the wondrous reality that is recovery.

In Fellowship,

Cecil C.